Looking Glass

A Fragmentized Reflection

Tomás Javier Colón

DEDICATION

To all of the pieces of this beautiful struggle I call life.

To the strength of my mother, the endless support of my wife, the warmth of my beautiful children, the unblemished solidarity of my little brother, the perseverance of my niece and my nephew, to the triumph of my two sisters in Jersey City, New Jersey, the guidance of my aunt and second mother, the fighting spirit of my uncle, the respect and trust of both my mother-in-law and father-in-law, the admiration of my sister-in-law and my brothers-in-law, the unforgettable memories of moments lived with my entire extended family in both Puerto Rico and Bronx, New York, the priceless advice of my wife's Grandmother, to those who watch over our entire family from the heavens, to my father for recognizing that there is still time to mend our hearts, to the courage of the men and women I served with, and to the winds that still carry the words and wisdom of someone I have never forgotten; keep smiling upon us Abuelita.

CONTENTS

PREFACE

There I stood, in front of the Christmas tree on the morning of the 25th of December and all I could do is ask myself how it was I let this holiday just come and go without putting a single gift under that tree. Everything about that morning just seemed well, a little off. New England temperatures at this time of the day are more often than not quite frigid. The sun was bright, blue skies, and the almost sixty degrees outside made it seem more like a down south Christmas. I felt inadequate as a father, a husband, and a provider. The deafening silence of a living room in a home which simply did not register on Santa's radar broke me. I quietly made myself a cup of coffee while thinking of the easiest way to tell my loved ones that their gifts would be just a little late this year however, that was not all that occupied my thoughts that morning. The payments on both our cars would be late, we had grown quite tired over the past couple of days of running through our DVD movie collection as our Cable TV service was interrupted due to non-payment, and I kept a watchful eye for the local utility company van who was due for a visit to disconnect our electrical power which had yet to be paid for. My wife and I have always worked yet we live in a constant worry about our bills. Thinking back, everything that morning just seemed more than just a little off. The question is not how does a good man get to this place as it is how does a good man stay in this place.

Being a father is quite a task. It is a task that many men in my generation have not taken to very well for so many unspoken reasons. Some of those reasons live so deeply entrenched in our personal experiences that it pains us to even reminisce about them. For some of us, this is exactly what motivates us to break the generational curse of the absent father phenomena and strive to become exceptional fathers. While others never seem to find the courage to break that cycle and appear to be quite content to simply conform to the long established norm. Becoming a good father requires much strength and commitment. My father wasn't involved most of my young life as he and my mother parted ways shortly after my brother was born. His absence in that crucial part of our lives left me with a void in certain parts of my childhood memories; I imagined him at certain events in my mind as if that was my own way to self soothe in order to minimize the pain and uncomfortableness. I wondered, even as a child, about what kind of father I would be when it was my turn. Even as I wrestled with so many questions and concerns about how it was that I would give that which I experienced very little of, within my own thoughts I stumbled upon the answer. I would give my children exactly what I wanted in a father.

The absolute importance of adult male figure in the home has been quite undervalued from my perspective. I have heard it said on more than occasion, "I don't need a man to help me raise my child"; I would venture to bet that most children experiencing the absence of a father don't share that same opinion. There was nothing more I wished for when I was a child than my father coming back home to stay with us for good. My mother did the very best that she could in providing for and supporting my younger brother and I, but there are just some lessons that a father must teach a son.

The absence of those lessons was made more bearable by hanging on to a pleasant memory that remains incredibly lucid even today. It was just after 7 am one summer morning when mom woke me. Mom dressed me in a pinstripe jumpsuit, a Thomas the Train tee-shirt, and a little train conductor hat. My father was on his way to pick me up; it was bring your son to work day at the Matchbox warehouse where my Father worked. My father arrived in his green Datsun 210 to pick

me up and off we went to the Matchbox warehouse. I had never seen

so many toys under one roof; I was the envy of my friends later that

afternoon. I returned home with more matchbox toys than I could

count. Dad let me have whatever toy I wanted from the warehouse and

he made sure that together we would pick some great toys for my

younger brother as well. I recall being so truly elated that day. During

our drive home from that warehouse, I seemed to have forgotten all

about the wonderful toys I was bringing home for my little brother and I

simply stared at Dad the whole way home. I hoped he was back for

good. I wished he would stay; I will never forget how much I hoped that

day would not have come to an end.

I had not seen him for a number of years when my brother said

to me one day, "Hurry, Dad is at the house and he wants to see you

too." I was just returning to school from a field trip to the Bronx Zoo

when I was caught by complete surprise by Dad's visit that day. We ran

down to the street we lived on and Dad was talking with Mom a little

further down the street in the old parking lot opposite St. Anthony's

High school. We held one another that day. While in his embrace that

day, for the first time I knew what it felt like to let something you loved dearly simply slip away. I knew he wasn't go to stay. I knew I would not see him ever again. Watching him drive off that day hurt like nothing I could ever explain.

There were so many moments in my life that seemed to always remind me of his absence; life's callousness does not discriminate against age. There were graduations, award ceremonies, and school plays to which he simply never arrived. I will always remember looking around the room hoping that he would be out there somewhere looking back at me with a smile. I never stopped looking for him out there. There were always two smiles in the room that comforted me always. At everything I ever did, there she stood with a gleam in her eye that would make any star in the night sky feel inadequate. Next to her was a little guy who always seemed to be in awe of everything I did no matter how small. My mother and my little brother were and still remain an incredible emotional support system in my life. We alone know the intricate details of the struggles we endured together. I always wondered how it would have turned out if Dad had stuck it out and stayed with us.

Mom worked from factory to factory wherever and whenever she found an opportunity. She would get up every morning at 5:00 a.m. and make breakfast for us. There was no way she was leaving without ensuring she left us something to eat fully prepared and on the table. That was and still is my beautiful mother; she puts her two boys first always. I witnessed the incredible strength of the human spirit through her willingness to remain standing through her struggle. Her pride was immeasurable. She never let on to anyone outside our home that we struggled immensely at times. There were moments in our struggles when she would sit in the window with a small cup of fresh brewed coffee and a cigarette. She cried while sitting at that window. I would stand silently behind her and watched the cigarette smoke and her tears go in opposite directions as if they had passed each other by on some lonely highway without ever knowing they shared the same sad point of origin. She never felt me standing there wishing she didn't have to go through this. Though the brunt of our obstacles she negotiated without the help of a dedicated husband and father to her children, she has done and continues to do such an incredible job.

Two thing we were never short of at home was love and hope. Not every moment of my childhood was saturated in despair and sadness. We were blessed with an extended family that we found many an opportunity to unite with as the adults would have get-togethers where the music and laughter made worries vanish almost instantaneously. Our family really loved to come together around endless amounts of those comfort foods that define the Puerto Rican culture. Our aunts, uncles, and cousins from Bronx, New York always found time to pay us a visit. Whether spending time at our house or an outing to Lake Welch, hanging out with the whole family always filled me with so much happiness. I have managed hold onto those memories of moments spent with my mother, brother, aunts, uncles, cousins, and friends as those moments shared helped shape the person that I have become today.

Today I have learned to gracefully accept that I am the sum of my life's experiences. I look at life through the eyes of a humble man who learned very early on that all of the human emotions we experience have a very particular manner of shaping our personality. How we deal with love, hate, hurt, acceptance, rejection, anxiety, separation, relationships, marriage, family, parenting, and an ever changing society is deeply rooted in all those emotions experienced through everyone and everything that has made an impact in our lives.

1

SOCIETAL REFLECTIONS

Rumba By The Colgate Clock (An outing with Uncle Pablo)

Hours before noon
Sun already high and bright
In a cloudless sky
Endless waves of chatter
Familiar language
Spanglish

Air filled with enticing scents
Fried foods
Comfort foods that define the culture
Of the beloved island we surely miss
Oh the sweet smell
Bacalaitos Fritos!

I pull the sweat soaked dollar from my pocket
Mami gave it to me for helping her this morning
Tunnel vision takes over as my nose
Follows the scent
I'm on my way
Bacalaitos were two for a dollar

Laughter is everywhere
Today's reason to fiestar
It's Independence Day
As the mind resorts to thinking righteously
I ask myself who's Independence we celebrate
It fades to the sound of Congas as
They are joined by the bongos
A loud voice announces
"Ruuumbaaa by the Colgate Clock"

Before I reach the bacalaitos
My dollar I exchange

Simply could not resist the smell
Piece of bread in one hand
Pincho in the other
Pushing through the crowd again
I want to see the rumba

Hay fuego en el veintitrés- sings the sonero
Percussionist play to perfection
As we hear the sound of the campana
Everyone is watching intently
The fiesta has only started
Hands clapping
People smiling
Worries are forgotten
If only for a brief moment

Rumba by the Colgate Clock
Music has not stopped
Ice cold cervezas flow deeper than the Hudson
As the adults partake in the golden cure
It's what makes them numb to everyday struggle
La rumba continues as a circle is formed
In the middle
A man and a woman

Walking to the beat of this intense soneo
They stare each other down
The man with cigarette in hand with his Soulful dance
Circles this morena de piel canela
She smiles playfully as everyone cheers with the beat
Pa pa pa, pa pa
La morena begins her dance

I look on and I am breathless
It feels as if we are back home on the island
Sun begins to set
The man and this morena drenched it sweat
Dance a dance that cannot be taught
It is a dance born of one's attitude and one's soul

A dance born of the cultural explosion of three worlds
She becomes quite sassy as the crowd chants
Ave Maria,   morena...

Fireworks explode into the night sky
The rumba continues uninterrupted
While some reflect on independence
Others quite content to stay slaves to the rhythm
And the scents of Borinquen's culture
The percussion begins to slow its pace
The crowd begins to share memories they hold
Of those they love and miss
Smiles turn to tears
As the rumba makes way to an emotion filled bolero

Those who are saddened in this sea of familiar faces
Are comforted instantaneously
We will not let another suffer alone
Embraces are exchanged
The bolero begins to find an end
Hearts begin to mend
The morena hastens her dance

Ice cold beer flows deeper than the Hudson
It drowns the trouble seas of sadness
Hands once again begin to clap
The voices again begin to chant
Ave Maria, morena

Lost in this familiar crowd
I dance to find my dance
One day I will be the man in the middle
Looking at mi morena face to face
As people look on and forget their pain
The smell of the bacalaitos
The tender pork of the pinchos
The Congas and the bongos
Will call me once more to this
Rumba at the Colgate Clock...

Courtesy of Miss Harris

Seven a.m. on an empty stomach
Mom and I
Slowly descend the stairs
Someone in our building
At some table
Sits behind a plate
On which sits the bacon
Whose smell danced
Mockingly into my flared nostrils
We had neither
Time nor bacon;   both
Absent commodities
Courtesy of Miss Harris

We prayed she
Had been fired
The sun had risen
Bringing with it
A sense of hope
Mom and I hoped
The last four dollars
In her pocket book
Would serve us well
Path train to and from
Journal square
Where we envisioned
Speaking to someone
Who cared enough
To fix our dilemma
An empty refrigerator
Uncertain as to

Whether or not
Our evening will be one of
Pleasant conversation
Over dinner
Or an intimate rendezvous
With hunger
Courtesy of Miss Harris

As the train darts out of
That dark tunnel
Minutes away from our stop
We still prayed
She had somehow been fired
Now we walk
Mom clutches her purse
As she shares her dream
Of my little brother and I
Being better
Of how much she dreams
Of he and I never
Having to take this walk
For these reasons

Mom always fought
To ensure her little boys
Were ok
Looking down at the
Cement steps
Decorated with flattened
Wads of gum and stains
Of what could be
Either the spilled coffee of
Late case workers
Dashing up to work or
The spit of disillusioned
Citizens leaving empty handed
Vowing once again
To never return to this
"Damn welfare department"

That just didn't "give a shit
About nobody"
We prayed and we hoped
She wasn't sitting at her desk

Up the elevator
Mom and I
In silence
The doors open
We step out leaving behind
The scent of cheap perfume
And cigarettes
Down the hallway we walked
Walls adorned with posters
Pictures of happy families
Hung haphazardly
Just barely hanging on
To the dingy walls
Just barely hanging on
Perhaps the reason why
No one would ever accuse
This place of
False advertisement

Into the office we walk
A sea of case workers
Buried in case files
Ears peppered
By the colorful insults
Of all of those who didn't
Receive a check yesterday
Our prayers however
Unanswered
There she sat
Uninterested and stoic
Miss Harris

It was my perception
That she genuinely

Did not care for those
Who went without
We were all parasites
Looking for a handout
She was notorious for
Losing people's files
Or not submitting them
On time as they would die
Somewhere in or on
Her desk
That's why mom and I
Once again were there
Courtesy of Miss Harris

Serving as an interpreter
I pleaded our case
On my mother's behalf
I sat through this
Uncaring and quite hurtful
Discourse undoubtedly
Uttered over and over again
At so many others
Who sat mired in despair
Before her
Looking for a glimpse of
Compassion

Out the window I stared
My mother sat
Stewing in anger
As her words disappeared
Into my ears
Never fully reaching that place
In which I could discern
Her meaning
When I finally stood on
My two feet
I looked at her
Without any hesitation

And gave her
That which she had
Coming to her
For such a long time

Even today I cannot recall
Where, how the words met
In my young mind
To form the phrases
That no other adult
Could muster
To let Miss Harris know
What a soulless being
She truly was
With security hustling
To reach her desk
The supervisor staring at me
Silence fell over the whole floor

I made them all aware
Mom and I were there
Because we simply had
No other recourse
The shame we felt
Depending on the state
Was more than enough
We were good people
The unfair treatment
I insisted was to end
Right then and there

My words, my voice
Was heard
Security guards surprisingly
Apologetically escorted us
To a different desk
To a case worker who's
Still remembered why
She became a caseworker

Our file was reviewed
Immediately approved
Dinner would not evade us
Not that evening

I learned at the age of twelve
To be courageous
To be strong for those I loved
Courtesy of Miss Harris...

Hip-Hop

You greeted my every mornin'
Toothbrush doubled as a Mic,
Bathroom mirror rattling to banging beats
Ill rhymes
Hard Times

You told our story
Vinyl, tape deck, Walkman
Headphones hidden under a black hood
Boots meet the concrete
Every step in unison with a dope beat

Listening to the Mic check
one two one two
You were always on time
Lost myself in every rhyme

Familiar to me the story they tell
This is life
Ghetto eloquent tales of heaven and hell
Even when I thought I walked alone
I still had you
Faithful and always true

Started this journey in the rain
Kept my head up
Boots beat the concrete till my sky was blue
I am just one voice of many yelling
Hip Hop we miss you...

Aspiring Writers Block

Who will these words touch?
In what manner will they grasp
The intended meaning behind
What I am trying to say?

Don't have much of an education
If I must say;
To have the little bit I do have
Is a blessing-
It's just enough to get me
Through a troublesome day.

The world is occupied with too much.
It's good for the soul to know
Of a simple man who writes not
To bewilder or twist the mind
Instead,
It's simply your heart he'd like
To touch.

I write of those things
Most at some point
Have felt inside;
Words not meant to impress or amaze
I'd never pretend to be the intellectual kind
I find it is a blessing to say what I feel
To feel what I say
If by this I live,
I should never have to hide.

I should never be mentioned in the same breath
As Hughes, Poe, Frost, or Angelou;
For their mastery of this craft
 in all of its complexities
forever surpasses my humble ability

In patience, time, and of course wisdom.
Myself, maybe I've just got a bit of a start.
I think I'll turn out quite fine
If like them,
I always write
Straight from the heart.

No Longer a Stranger

Your hair is a mess
Face unshaven
Should I pretend you are less
Your likeness quite graven

Your scent is offensive
Even from afar
Yet I'm left quite pensive
As to who you truly are

You held out your hand
Asked for spare change
I'll give what I can
This seemed a bit strange

Your saddened eyes
Hide so much pain
The unheard cries
Again you've slept in the rain

Dreams of a decent meal
A warm place to sleep
Your misfortune is real
Seeds of hurt buried deep

So much comes to mind
But what shall I do
I'm compelled to make time
To simply listen to you

How could life be so unfair?
No one cares you exist
We all walk pass you and stare

This morning it is I that insist

I need to know your story
How did this come to be?
Days were once filled with glory
This could one day be me

Clearly fallen from grace
No old friends insight
Who would recognize your face
If you called to them tonight

I sit with you dear friend
Your pain with me please share
Your struggle needs an end
Today you'll know I care

You hang your head in shame
No reasons to smile
I'm thankful you came
And just spoke for a while

You are far from a burden
A remarkable man
One thing is certain
I'll never forget that you shook my hand

Cursed To Know

Books Educate
A history of disappointment
Within my heart
The ill sentiments
Of those who came before me
Once again replicate

Knowledge is pain
When it paints
Years of injustice
Psychological conditioning
Societal oppression by design
Cause of a piercing disdain

Waking up to lies
Truth shouts
From behind shades of gray
Wanting to be heard
Needing to be looked upon
By the purest of eyes

The road is long
Searching for a time
In which human appreciation
For one another's struggles
And one another's triumphs
Is all but gone.

Restless (the beating of war drums)

In the stillness of night
 We lay to rest
 Drifting to the sound of
 The cricket's melody;
 An owl interrupts just briefly.
 Though he has done so
 Every night,
 Tonight I am aware.
 How truly fortunate
 That I can enjoy
 A certain sense of safety
 As so many others
 Live gripped by fear.
 On the other side of the world
 They will not know sleep.
 The cricket's melody
 replaced by
 The sound of bombs.
 The deafening cries of children
 Interrupting just briefly;
 They are aware.
 Unsure if their eyes
 Will rest upon a majestic sunrise,
 Or upon the stillness of
 The dead bodies of
 Men, women, and children.
 Lifeless   children,
 Who like us
 In the stillness of night
 Once lay to rest.
 Drifting to the sound of
 The cricket's melody,
 Peace becomes a memory

Silenced by the drums
Of war.
God have mercy on us
For the legacy of
We leave and
For these ignorant reasons
We continue
to take lives for.

Better Days

This journey ever changing
Countless twists and endless turns
So many of us give up the struggle
We still have so much to learn

This life has yet to be easy
Obstacles come and go
Enough tears to form a river of hope
Sweet waters flow through
Streams we have yet to know

Tired of simply treading water
Chasing dreams that fade away
Reaching out with empty palms
Waiting for my share of that better day

Holding on to those we love
Together we get past the pain
Open up your heart
Shelter someone through their rain

Meet me at the crossroads
Take my hand and walk with me
Better days just off the horizon
This dream so lucid yet still
So very hard to see.

2

Manhood: Under Construction

A Barstool, a Bottle, and Time

All I need is-
A barstool,
A bottle, and
Time
To reflect on
What I have become

I only wish
To numb this
Pain
That eats away
Without regard
For my forlorn
Existence

I fault no one
For benefiting
From my altruistic
Nature;
Without ever expecting
To sit here
With nothing left to give and,
Alone
I put all those
I deeply loved
Before all I ever
Dreamed

Now as you all
Have grown and changed,
Your disdain leaves me feeling
Insignificant-
As I have nothing but

My heart and my hopes
Which is clearly not
Enough
For you to remember-
 I was motivated by Love
To ensure my family's
Survival.

Today, believing
I have, in you, a helping hand
I stand in these walls of
Silence
Hoping only for-
A barstool,
A bottle,
And time
To numb the
Pain...

Calculated Existence

Standing still
All goes by
At blinding speeds
Hour hand
Marks time
So quickly
It makes
Minute hands
Travel like seconds
While the hand of seconds
Is rendered obsolete
It falls from the
Face of time and
Drops into
The palm of my hand
A more familiar place
Trying to slow time just enough
Attempting to stay relevant
Hoping someone would stop
And notice me trying
Trying to weave my thoughts
Into the fabric of time
Breath
Slowly
Deliberately
It all comes to fruition
Through patience
Appreciate every second
Even if all seems to
Pass you by
In a hurried pace
Build a story
Worth remembering

One Second at a Time...

Feel Me?

Thoughts arise from my soul
To be expressed in the simplest of terms,
How else am I to elaborate on-
A life full of pain as I utter those
Oh so colorful words of discontent?
Feel me if you too have walked in these tired shoes...

How arrogant of me to hide
My meaning in complex words and phrases
When your generosity compelled you
To grant me a moment of your precious time,
Feel me if your soul has ever known the blues...

Look at me smile as if life could never
Find a way to be unfair
As I could recall, leaving that city block
And becoming a man of any importance
Was a distant thought
I still persevere, I know you are out there,
Feel me, if to laying down you too refuse...

My heart has known the pain of living in "Almost"
Almost able to be someone,
Almost able to live the dream
Comfort and sheer bliss have eluded me
Because of who and what I am
When I get there
I still won't put it on cruise,
I know you are out there
Feel me?

Nothing

Nothing that I do matters
I was born from a history of insignificance
Cardboard cutouts of dreams that
Return to a state of nonexistence
After the violent rain of this
Never-ending storm that defines
My life

I give all that I have
All that I am
Yet, inadequate is the only adjective
That seems to best describe
What I thought was my best
A painful reminder of who I really truly am
I am nothing .

This charade of being regarded as
He whose sole purpose is
To break this cycle of remaining
An unknown soul to this world
Is nothing more than that
A masquerade that has
Carried on for much to long
I am consumed by shame

I dressed myself of love and sacrifice
As I offered, all that I was,
All that I hoped to be
How erroneous of me to expect
That to be enough
I am to never forget
That underneath it all
I am and always will be

To you and to this world
Nothing

Born of a history of insignificance
Forever doomed to live out
The story of a man who
Dreamed of meaning something
To someone who from time to time
Strips me down to nothing
Achieving only one thing
Reminding me of the very thing that I fear the most,
That I will only ever be

Nothing...

Pain is a Place

With chairs in a circle
my first thought-
I wasn't supposed to be here

Heart starts to race
Temperature elevated
Readying my vein for this poetic fix

Such anticipation, this
Emotional game of —"duck duck goose"
All eyes on me
As if I were Tupac Shakur and this was 1996

A poem of triumph— perhaps,
An ode to the spirit of Herbert Gans.
Pulling myself up by the bootstraps
trying to escape the chains of hard luck

Maybe even a poem of choices
deciding on one of two roads like Robert Frost
Even if my pen bled of this,
No one would really give a fuck.

Is it an absolute that pain sells?
Is human hurt the only thing that moves you?
I still struggle to believe this is the case
In my world,   pain is a place
Pain is that place where-
Dad walks out and never looks back
No one hears your cries
Summer vacations are non-existent
Dinner is a small bowl of plain white rice

A weekly salary at the age of nine

Four years and still no birthday card from Dad…

Mom's tears run deeper than the Hudson,
Her face enveloped by the smoke of Newport cigarettes;
she was the portrait of a woman scorned.
Her curse,
I look just like him.

High school days full of haze

Escaped reality with Mary Jane.

Thirteen years and still no birthday card from Dad…

My first attempt at college lasted only one lecture.
Success was— shipping out to boot camp
Missing your own child's first steps
Walking on unfamiliar soil in the name of "peace"
A world away from all you love
Barely making out an "I miss you" over a bad phone connection
Having a needle inserted into your arm while sitting next to an addict
Selling plasma from my blood for twenty-five dollars a visit
Rushing home in a daze with baby formula for a crying child

Eighteen years and still no birthday card from Dad…

An almost failing marriage
Getting into a car full of rage
Almost giving in and becoming what you most despise
Seeing their smiles, hearing their laughter for maybe the last time
A lonely stairwell that echoed their cries
Searching for ways to always provide
A paycheck big enough to only tread water
Week equivalent to forty hours of work, eighty hours of school

Breaking the promise of a sweet sixteen to a daughter;
In my world pain is a place.

Here I am baring my very soul
Opening my closet
Some say my courage has seen me through
I wasn't supposed to be here with you

Thirty three years and still no birthday card from Dad —

Pain is a place…

Procrastination

Whiskey swirls in my glass
Broken only by two rocks
Keep cool, help me forget the past
Music stopped long ago
All I hear is the ticking of the clock
The mind fights to take flight
Feet stay glued to the ground
Time stands so still tonight
As absurd as this sounds
I simply pour myself another drink
Gray hairs set in
All I do is sit and think
But I will never share what lies deep within
So alone in this place
If you wonder what pains me
Read between the lines of this old weathered face
Could've, would've, and should've
Held me down like the roots of a tree
Whiskey swirls in my glass
Broken only by two rocks
Sound never subsides
Tick Tock Tick Tock
This life passed me by much too fast

Questioning Misdirection

When my pen touches the paper
Fingers begin to pulsate
Arms stiffen and get tense
My body temperature rises.

My eyebrows descend;
The space between comes together
Marking a short trail
A short trail of long disappointment-
My nostrils flare
Anger stirs deep inside me.

This struggle to never lose hope
Slipping through my fingers;
The path of inhumanity
More frequently traveled
Than that of the path of humanity.

Rage flows through my veins
A sense of a brighter tomorrow-
Overshadowed by disbelief;
Hopelessness on paper
Words that echo:
The pain of a battered woman,
The lifeless body of an abused child,
Unhinged by the frailty of the starving;
A jobless man prepares a noose

Enraged by the stoicism of politicians.

As we are collectively lulled to sleep,
We gain ground ever so quickly
Inevitable this collision course
With modern day slavery;
This poem may end up--
A mere rant about where we are
As a society.

Insignificant words of a common man
Fueled by a thirst to understand,
One simple question—

Why?

Resignation

Hardship greeted me with open arms
Gray monochrome rainbows remain
Blessed in the waters of misfortune
Surely baptized by Saint Someday

Gray monochrome rainbows remain
I've grown so tired of chasing
Surely baptized by Saint Someday
"Almost" stands forever in the way

I've grown so tired of chasing
Blessed in the waters of misfortune
"Almost" stands forever in the way
Hardship greeted me with open arms

Serenity

If only life
Would find it prudent
To allow tranquility
To reach me
If even once in a great while
The brevity of that peace
Would suffice
In being that memory
I could revisit
In order to live it
With a smile

Storms

Relentless storms
Awakening despair
Waves of troubles
Overcome the sands
As the shores of
A once content heart
Are simply erased
From the landscape
Of a place called
Hope

The white dove
Flees
Leaving no trace
Of a brief visit
Hands outstretched
Palms raised
To no avail
New beginnings
Welcomed with such
Measured despair
Hidden behind
A forced smile

Seems life
Finds a way
To divert a
Path full of
False security
Towards one
Of fulfilment

Navigating around
Relentless Storms
Has only kept them
Raging
In the center.

Time

Have you simply passed me by?
For me you surely did not wait
Oh how I wish that I could fly
It was you I've squandered as of late

Two hands do tell your tale
If I could merely slow you pace
My plans have grown quite stale
Soon I too shall leave this place

So many words have gone unspoken
Making ill use of you, my crime
Promises will go broken
Another notch upon your line

To Those I Hold Dear

How I wish I could please those I love
Without losing touch with me
I envy the beautiful dove
If only I were that free

High are the expectations
What ever shall I do?
Consumed by such trepidation
I hope never to bid you adieu

You all hold a place in my heart
Understand I long for tranquility
The absence of tolerance tears me apart
My love alone has not been formidable enough to bring unity

My sanity depends on your coming together
That which bonds family is forever

3

LOVE'S TOLL

From Comfort

When all came asunder
Colors faded and grew tired
Sanity all but flees
You, held me

Certainty's solidity is breeched
Questions wage war
Thoughts deep like the yellow on the flowers
Born of Black Eyed Susan
You simply listened quite intently

Tears descend tired cheeks
Their path broken by quivering lips
Salt from lonely oceans I taste
You said nothing as you held me

A life full of burden
I lay my head upon your shoulder
Whispers of hope you uttered
Through the darkness you kept me company

Inside these lonely walls
In a dark and lonely space
Trapped by Winter Jasmine
You rescued what was left of me.

A Moonlit Sky for You and I

Sensual light of a moonlit sky
Traveling through the ages
To simply find an open window
From which it may contemplate
How we exchange thoughts of
Passion and Love

Without pronouncing
A single word
Never growing tired
Holding one another
We lay together
In this dimly lit room
Staring at the moonlit sky

Hold forever that twinkle in your eyes
For even as my body grows tired and old
This burning desire to be near you,
It never seems to subside

Hurts to Love

I have felt
Both love and pain
They weigh the same
Equal in intensity
One awakens the senses
The other erodes the soul
All the same
The will to continue,   fades
As bright colors
Turn to dull shades
I long to feel neither

The strength and intellect
Needed to decipher
Which of these will be the victor
In one's heart
Has fallen
Like the sunset over the horizon
As the stars brighten the
Night sky

Let me sleep so still
Utter not the words
"I love you";
All I ask in return
For all the love
I have given
Unconditionally-
Be silent dear love

Let me drift into eternity
Without asking
Why loving you simply hurts;
Without asking
Why you chose to make me feel
Unappreciated

Love and pain
Both weigh the same
One awakened my senses
As the other eroded my soul
My will has faded
Bright colors
Turned to dull shades

Let me drift
I've no longer the strength
To pretend
That I no longer feel
How much it truly hurts
To love.

I Forget

The day this world was gifted with your existence
Fortune had passed me by.
I was not the first man to hold you
Nor did I hear your first cry.

I don't contemplate it much,
I would much rather forget.
While I struggle to accept that it was out of my control,
For it is the one thing I regret.

I forget-
It was simply not I who greeted you into this life;
When he chose to walk away from you
Your mother became my wife.

The universe finally noticed me.
You were so very little when you first looked me in the eye.
I picked you up in my arms and just held you;
I promised to be the best father I could be to you until the day I die.

Over the years I forget
Because the bond we share is strong.
You are my son and I your father;
Who will ever dare say that we are wrong?

Every milestone in your life is engrained in my heart.
I've kissed you good night, tucked you in,

And even healed your scars.
Now although you have become
Quite the responsible young man,
I am here for you always and I will never be too far.

I forget that I was not there in the very beginning,
You will never imagine how much I wish that
The privilege of being there was mine to be had.
Just know forever that I will never walk away from you,
 Because you chose to call me Dad.

Memories of You

Quite often I revisit
Those tender moments
That never seem to fade away
My subconscious gently rocks
You have anchored what was us
Forever in my mind
The tides come and go
You remain
Refusing to go ashore
Quietly sitting
Readying your bait
In the middle of my thoughts
Your sweet kiss
Along with the memories
Of indulging in the feel
Of your perspiring skin
The intoxicating smell of
Your brown hair
Forever lures me to that hook
Caught forever
At the mercy of
Those memories
That set my mind adrift
To that space in time
The hurt of your lies
Was rendered numb
Whenever we made love
Whispers of hollow words
Memories of loving you
Failing to accept
That in your journey
Into forever
My existence is but insignificant
Yet the memories of you

Remain anchored in my
Thoughts
As the tides come and go…

Only You

A Sweet kiss from
Your Rose colored lips
Is the switch that turns on
The blue sky in my world

Your "Good Morning" and
"I Love you"
Enunciated with that Spanish accent
My morning song

The scent of your cinnamon skin
Renders the wild red columbine obsolete
As the hummingbirds gather at our window
They too are attracted to your beauty

With just a brief message that reads
"I Miss You"
You send my heart above the clouds
Higher than the Sun
On a summer afternoon

The evening draws closer
I can already sense the scent of your hair
Like wild ginger
So sweet
Anxiety claims its victory over me
I just can't wait to get home to you

Under the covers
With you in my arms
Whether making love
Or making believe we are wide awake
I could never drift into
Pleasant dreams without you

A Sweet kiss from
Your Rose colored lips
Is the switch
To the gentle breeze underneath my moonlit sky.

Parting Ways

Let your heart speak
Whatever it may feel
Be it joyous or even bleak
It tells of what's real

Hide not your intention
Be forthcoming and true
Avoid all circumvention
I would still respect you

If our love is no more
We should honorably part
Let me walk out the door
With an ounce of my dignity and what's left of my heart

Promise

When the sky begins to fade
My eyes find the darkness
This beating heart halts
The sound of nothingness takes with it
Everything we never had the chance to say
Just when I cease to be,
Promise that you won't
Kiss me...

When the cold is upon me
This pulse that once quickened at the very sound of your voice
Now echoes in a space where you can't follow
When all I know ceases to be
Just hold my hand
Don't kiss me

When we become a memory
Just when my soul begins that journey
For which none of us prepare,
It would be eternally cruel
To know I had no choice
Returning to your lips
A fruitless wish
If you love me
Understand how that would
Kill me, once more

Promise that you won't

Kiss me; I could not bear
The thought of
Never returning
To the tenderness
Of your rose colored
Lips;
Promise

Still In Love

Years have passed
Season after season
This body has also changed
This soul still loves you the same

Winds have blown
Sands travel many an hourglass
Time left its mark upon my face
Nothing can match your embrace

For years I have watched the sunrise
I've held you through many a sunset
My youth slowly slips away
Yet, I want you more than I did yesterday

Hold my hand the whole way through
Gray hairs and wrinkled skin
Of making love to you I'll never tire
This flame forever burns simply because it was you who lit the fire

The I in Irony

I remember mornings with you
Waking up in your embrace
Inspired a feeling of invincibility
For once, things had fallen into place

The smell of fresh brewed coffee
Dancing through the air
Had fallen quite short in comparison
To the smell of your brown hair

Today remembering those mornings,
Is what my existence has been reduced to
I resent the smell of coffee
Just as much as I hate you

Your departure unwarranted and abrupt
Left me anchored in a sea of vulnerability
Condemned to lonely mornings in utter silence
Permanently deprived of love's tranquility

For if another finds a brief shelter
In the lies of your embrace
I know that soon enough I'll share their company
Indefinitely in this lonesome place

Tracks

Stale morning air
Knots in my stomach
Lump in my throat
Keeps me silent
Words have become-
Useless
These tracks will
Forever signify
Your departure
Trains whistle rings
Reminding me
It's much too late
The rumbling
Makes the ground shake
Though my legs
Were immersed in that
Sensation long before
The train made its
Dreadful approach
I stand idly by
Not knowing what
To say
These tracks will lead
You away
From my heart
Steam fills the station
We embrace
And say nothing

You disappeared into
The steam
And boarded the train
As these tracks
Took you away
I stand in mist
This lonely morning
Finally finding
The words to say
"Please stay...."

Winter's Breath

Cold morning-

Winters' breath never subsides;
Beating against an old window
The dreadful rattling of glass,
Held against its will.

Half a century old this wooden window frame-
A life of ups and downs,
Rolling hills of virgin snow,
Like a photo; rendered timeless.
Simply to offer admiring eyes an image
Esthetically pleasing,
Unless of course,
You dare open the window.

Now all becomes tangible.
Overcome by winters breath,
I think of us.
I ponder what it is that we've become.

Warmth departs;
I feel as if I've fallen into nothingness,
An ocean of your kisses-
So cold.

If only warmth would return
I shut this old wooden framed window
Return to simply gazing at these rolling hills
The beauty of the virgin white snow-
Framed,

Only offering admiring eyes an image.

We are that beauty that lives outside the window;
We have become just an image,
An image of what love appears to be-

Aesthetically pleasing,

Absent tangibility,

A closed window-

As I utter the words "I love you"
They are muted by
The dreadful rattling of glass
Held against its will.

All but succumbing
To winters' breath.

4

A REBIRTH

Awakening

Looking up
To the heavens
The energy that
Is my soul
Awakens,

The energy that is
My soul
Vaguely recalls
Dancing
Out there
Somewhere
Seeking enlightenment.

The birth of
My soul
In this vessel
In this place
A test of will power
Presumably,

To endure in silence
While experiencing how
Palpable
The inhumanity of
Humanity
Has truly become.

Deja vu placed
In a sealed box
Out of reach
In the depths

Of conscious thought
Slowly escapes
Allowing only small
Fragments
Of an undeniable
Truth.

Looking up
To the heavens
I am overwhelmed
The energy within me
Stirs
Uncontrollably
The soul is
Prepared
Yet the mind
May not comprehend,

We have all
Danced
In places where
Love and compassion
Knows no limits
Out there where-
The energy that is
The soul
While embracing
A shooting star
Will race across the
Night sky
Hoping to hear
A child's wish.

Existence
Is not a gift
To be squandered;
Feed the soul
Nourish the mind

Seek out the purpose
Of your time,

Resist the lies
Of conformity
When the energy
That is your soul departs
To that place
It's only company
Will be,
The Labor of
Love or
Hate
You left behind-

Looking up
To the heavens
The energy that
Is my soul
Awakens...

Omnipotence of Thought

Gentle winds move
Words spoken, forever carried
Be mindful of what escapes you to have been forged in love
Blissful thoughts move in tandem with these gentle winds

Ill-fated speak rises from the darkness of an evil heart
Forged in hate and envy
Baneful suppositions disturb placid winds
Blue skies depart overwhelmed by gray

Cold rain dances uncertain in quivering winds
Storms approach celebrating generous helpings of lament
Thoughts are of miscalculated omnipotence
Be mindful of what escapes you to be forged in love

Enlightened (A Soap Box Spiritual)

I am,
I am he who
As a child clung
To hope
I am he who
Knew sadness
As he who made me
Walked, faded
I am he
He who walked through
The doors of
Public schools
To learn or
Better yet
Be force fed
The bullshit
That this system
Wanted me to ingest
In order to maintain
The status quo
Another Rican
Up at the crack
Of dawn
Racing off to
Lackawanna
Or even
Port Jersey Boulevard
Factory work extraordinaire
—That's all they
Wanted me to know
I am
I am he
Who was never

Supposed to know
Anything other
Than the
Dingy white walls
Of a railroad
Apartment
In the brick building
That I grew up in
I am he
Who blazed
A trail of possibilities
So that my
Seed
Could fly higher
Than I
I am
A husband
A father
A son
A brother
A student
Of life
Who gives every
Damn ounce
Of what makes
Me who I am
To those
I love
Only hoping
That long after
I am gone
They will
See
That I conquered
Every obstacle
That I smashed
Every stereotype
Just to prove
I exist

I am
I am he
Who has laughed and
Has cried
He who has masked
The pain with a smile
I am he
Who keeps an
Open mind
Hoping one day
You will find
My soul
In every line
I have penned
With a tear in my eye
I am he
Who will never
Forget
From where he came
He who will never
Cease to seek truth
At times I am weak
When I feel like
Letting go
I write and I speak
Because
I Am.......

Let Me

Let me dance in hope
With my head held high
Forevermore
I simply want to be

Let me dream of better days
For even if they are miles away
Bind not my aspirations
My only obstacle is me

Let me live unscathed
By your ill judgment
Take a moment to hear
My voice tells a story of a people

Let me walk my path
I have overcome many hurdles
Fortune is for once being kind
Tranquility is on the horizon

Let me lay the foundation
Upon which my children will build
A future of promise
It is for them I beg of thee

Let me give unto them
The same you have given unto yours
Not a generational curse
But a generational hope.

Lessons

Life
One must live
Rest
One must sleep
Charity
One must give
Hope
One must keep

Heart
One must share
Children
One must teach
Empathy
One must care
Needy
One must reach

Laugh
One must smile
Dreams
One must chase
Helping
Is worthwhile
Warmth
One must share with
A caring embrace.

Through the Chains

Struggle binds the soul
Changing lanes swapping roles
Truth is
Always find myself in a hole

I am just a man
Not a man with a plan
From one dream to the next
Hanging off this cliff with one hand

Unremarkable past
How long will this nightmare last?
My American dream
Once a Soldier, still an outcast

Never owned a white picket fence
Others lose homes and live tense
160 hours only covers my rent
There's something about Peter and Paul that makes sense

Just need a little room to breath
My queen and my kids I'll never leave
Lace up my boots and I keep walking
It costs nothing to believe

just another face

Navigating a merciless place
Tell me again I won't make it
For you in my world there's no space

Hope is waking up every morning
Under the radar this nobody is soaring
Stereotypes I decimate
Your chains are not strong enough
Just a warning-

The March of Autumn

Tree tops like
An ocean of
Gold, brown, and fiery red
Sway silently
Along the countryside
In early autumn's chill
Leaves begin their descent
Letting go
Free Falling to a
Certain death

Comforted only
By a promise of
Rebirth

Lay silently
Ocean of
Gold, brown, and fiery red
In a brief moment
You will be
Simply a memory
Of another year
Marching undisturbed
Into yesterday.

The Poet

Emotions fuel
The desire to tell about
These moments
Love, Hate, Joy, and Pain
Their origin is quite the same
Born in a common place
If you should wonder which one I'm experiencing now
Simply gaze upon my face

Each day presents
Moments worth remembering
Accounts I attempt to make timeless
I put my pen to paper and my heart begins to overflow
So much to share
With those who dare to if only for a moment genuinely care
My hand begins the to and fro

There is simply no escape
It is just I and my emotions
Thoughts deeper than the ocean
I write

I write so that you know that I existed
I lived
I loved
I hurt
I healed
My pen still writes though at times my lips remain sealed

Hope is a precious commodity
These poems I leave behind so the world will know my humble
heart
Physically existing forever is an oddity.
My words can live on
Much after I'm gone
I shall blow out this candle and lay down to rest
Quickly approaching is dawn

Gratitude

For every sunrise
I am eternally grateful
I smile at you world
For this new day
I thank you Lord
Only you can give
this precious gift
Today I walk again
It is because of you that I
breathe the air I breathe
It is forever by your grace
That every sunrise
Is for me a new opportunity
A new beginning

A Poet Is Courageous

A poet is courageous.
The voice of truth
Pulling away the veil
Helping those who listen-
Realize that the lies,
Like two left sided shoes,
Will make it easy
To walk in circles

A poet is courageous;

A poet is courageous,
When he or she speaks to
Their own personal journey
You see-
I could spew angry indifference as
Newspaper headlines and
Main stream media
Incite hopelessness and despair;
So, unless you have walked
Alongside the tuberculosis ridden children of
Haiti and
Held on to those tiny little hands
That grew tired of
Holding on to hope
As they fade into yesterday,
Speak your truth!

Until you know the sound
Of mortar or artillery fire
When it rains down upon
A village and
Topples its houses like
A deck of cards;
The sound of bricks
Turning to rubble
As lives crumble.
Hope lost in the
Particles of dust that-
Linger within the smoke that
Dances amongst the
Deafening silence of
The innocent.
Speak your truth!

Speak of that which
Has tested your resolve,
That which when revisited
Takes you to that place where
Love picked up the broken pieces
That once made up your life,
That place where-
Hurt tore through every
Fiber of your being as you
Drowned in your tears.
Speak of that place where
Hope finally gave you
The strength to
Write through the pain or
Pic up a microphone and
Watch everyone hang on to
Your every word as

You feel that lump in
Your throat makes
Your voice crack and
your palms sweat because,
The reciting of a poem has
Become a recounting of
Of a story that
Is life,
Your life
Out on display.

A poet is courageous.
The voice of truth
Show us that
Taking off the veil
Allowed you to see
Our two left sided shoes
So then maybe
Poet
Just maybe,
We may all-

Stop walking in circles.

Whispers of Wisdom

It took me quite
a number of years to
unlearn all of the
macho bullshit
that in my first
20 years of life
made me believe
I fully understood what
it meant to be a man.
To comprehend what
the true essence
of what it truly means
to be a man,
I had to search deep
within me;
it was there that I learned
that in order to be
a good man,
one must first embrace
the beauty of
simply being
Hu-man.

ABOUT THE AUTHOR

Tomás Javier Colón earned a Bachelor's Degree in Sociology from Eastern Connecticut State University in Willimantic, CT. He is currently working as a Fathering Home Visitor where he gets to work in partnership with struggling fathers throughout the community in order to assist and educate them in regards to the importance of their roles as fathers. Together with his wife of 18 years he has raised four beautiful children. He is also a proud United States Army Veteran.

Made in the USA
Middletown, DE
03 April 2015